Stiletto Standards

WHAT EVERY WOMAN

NEEDS TO KNOW TO LIVE THE

LIFE OF HER OWN DESIGN

SUZANNE MALAUSKY

i

Stiletto Standards

WHAT EVERY WOMAN NEEDS TO KNOW
TO LIVE THE LIFE OF HER OWN DESIGN

Inquiries regarding permission for the use of material contained
in the book should be emailed to **suzanne@weinspirellc.com**
or addressed to:
   WeInspire, LLC
   1468 Network Drive
   Canonsburg, PA 15317

Printed in the United States of America

ISBN: 978-1-793-14258-0

CREDITS

COPY EDITOR
Elizabeth Pagel-Hogan
www.onesweetwriter.com

COVER DESIGN AND LAYOUT
Amy Glass Rajakovic
www.YellowBasedGreen.com

PHOTOGRAPHY
A-J Kyler Photography
Erin Beth Hollie
Michelle Burkett

DRESS FOR SUCCESS

Clothing, connections, confidence! The mission of Dress for Success is to empower women to achieve economic independence by providing a network of support, professional attire and the development tools to help women thrive in work and in life.

DRESS FOR SUCCESS®
PITTSBURGH

I have been drawn to the mission of Dress for Success for many years. The work of the organization and its volunteers has been the catalyst for countless inspiring and empowering stories around the world. This book is my opportunity to help women develop skills to realize personal success. It's also my opportunity to help with monetary support. **Ten percent of the proceeds of every copy of this edition of *Stiletto Standards* purchased will be donated to Dress for Success Pittsburgh** to help further their reach and depth of services.

LEARN MORE AT *pittsburgh.dressforsuccess.org*

TABLE OF CONTENTS

To be happy,
it first takes being comfortable
being in your own shoes.

~ SOPHIA BUSH

INTRODUCTION

Why Stilettos?

Shoes are a very important part of any wardrobe. Our shoes are what we choose to put on every day to navigate our way through the world. They are also the first thing we take off when we want to relax and unburden ourselves. We have so many choices of styles and colors and heel height. Just like we have choices about our attitude, what we learn, and how we act.

I chose the stiletto-style shoe as a symbol of femininity. To represent the fact that being feminine still has a place in feminism. It's also a metaphor for the idea that personal style - whatever yours might be - is a significant part of how we all walk through life.

The image of or thought of wearing stilettos may not be positive for everyone. They can be uncomfortable, old school, and may even seem a little slutty. But they are also provocative. They can represent an aspirational target for little girls who want to grow up and fit into mom's shoes. They can represent classic ideals for dress and behavior.

Stilettos also represent the idea that women do not have to dress or act like men to fit in or stand out. They represent the power of choice to wear whatever you want and to be whatever you want. In fact, the range of style choices we have as women is an underestimated advantage. So let's explore those styles instead of limiting ourselves.

The image of stilettos is eye-catching. But the message of Stiletto Standards is self-empowerment. You don't need to wear stilettos or even like stilettos – you need to do you. The key is to own your style and behavioral choices; to be comfortable, confident and capable of navigating life in the shoes of your choosing. Ballerina flats, combat boots, Birkenstocks or Jimmy Choo's, it's completely up to you.

Why Stiletto Standards?

I first wrote *Stiletto Standards* as a series of blog posts to explore and articulate my point of view on how modern women represent feminism. It was originally sparked by an observation that emerging female leaders in America's high-profile businesses and in American politics seemed to me to be more feminine. This seemed like a huge difference to me than female leaders from earlier decades.

This got me thinking. Was it somehow now more acceptable to be and act 'like a girl' to get ahead?

When I was younger, being a feminist meant being less feminine. Today, being a feminist represents freedom to be who you are. This also means you have to own who you are. You have to understand your choices may not fit with where you are and or get you where you want to be. You can show up for a job interview in your leopard-print rubber boots, but that doesn't mean you can't be upset when the hiring manager feels that you won't be a fit.

It isn't always about fashion, but the cold shoulder trend is a great example. One woman might hate it because she's always cold; another might love it because she's always overheated and it gives her some relief. There's no right or wrong here, there's just knowing yourself and understanding the variety of reactions you may get to your choices.

As I thought more and more about what women needed to be successful in the modern world, I identified ten standards. As women progress through their lives, these ten standards will help them as leaders of their families, businesses, communities, and more. In each section, I offer context, content, and applicable tips to help women build confidence in navigating life's challenges.

Now *Stiletto Standards* is a book. This is my little way of contributing to the evolution of women everywhere as we continue to explore the roles that women play in society and in their own success. My hope is some of this advice helps women define their standards for healthy choices that lead to their success.

I wrote those first blog posts ten years ago. In the time between their appearance on the internet and the publication of this book, the #MeToo movement has grown into a powerful and thought-provoking aspect of our modern world. To me, #MeToo represents a surge of energy in the women's movement. This includes men respecting women, and women respecting men. I asked myself, how can I help?

I'm not an expert on the women's movement; but I am a woman. I write this from my perspective, based on my experiences. It's the only lens I have to view the world. My sincere hope is to provide valuable tools to all kinds of women. I can't personally explain the perspectives of women from a variety of backgrounds and experiences. What I can do is welcome your feedback on how these tools have worked for women from all walks of life, from different races and ethnic groups, different sexual identities and religions, different physical and mental abilities.

In general, my perspective on life is built on how I can maintain a positive focus on the future and less on retribution for the past acts of others. I prefer more proactive efforts and fewer reactionary antics. So, what could I do to help reduce the need to dig up ghosts of bad behavior of the past? Could I help women to choose empowerment and accountability for themselves instead of demanding they be bestowed upon them by others?

I believe the energy we put into life comes back to us. Negative thoughts and behaviors lead to unmet dreams and unrealized goals. Positive energy results in greater satisfaction and success. It's one thing to tell people what to think, it's quite another, and a more impactful act, to teach, educate and change thinking habits from the inside out. So why not embrace an optimistic view of the work and people in it? Let's embrace the belief that we can change the human dynamic even if it's one person and one situation at a time.

Someone once said that you get treated the way you allow others to treat you. If you believe even partly in this sentiment, then why not be willing to examine the way you present yourself to others? Think about how you approach people and how you react to them as part of your personal success strategy. With more knowledge, a different perspective and the right skills, you can inspire new behaviors, constructive conversations, mutual respect and advocacy in others.

My goal is to help women be who they want to be, to define their own success without being limited by a lack of choices, self-confidence, or knowledge.

My contribution to the new women's movement, therefore, is to use my experience, research, and education to equip any woman with a point of view and an associated skillset, that when applied, enables her to experience the success that she alone defines.

•••

Baby, darling,

I am passionate about this!

If it intrigues you, challenges you,

haunts you—the activity or the

place—then you must have a go at it!

~ HELEN GURLEY BROWN

•••

How to Use This Book

I believe that women need three essential tools. They need self-knowledge, which includes an understanding of their strengths and vulnerabilities. They need access to a skillset that builds respect. And they need confidence to know when to apply their skills. With these three tools, women will be unstoppable. They will be able to take risks and bring about changes in interpersonal relationships, whether in the family, workplace, or community, that result in healthier dialogue and stronger relationships.

Throughout this book, I share some of my own personal anecdotes to illustrate a skill or mindset that I believe will help a woman live a life of her own design. I also share stories of other women who have walked a similar path and are working toward their own success. I encourage you to do the strategy assessments at the end of each chapter. Write directly in the book, in your journal, or on your device. Read more about the research that I've highlighted. Ask questions. Talk about your ideas and concerns with your network. And don't forget to get in touch with me and share your insights. I want to hear your stories, too.

Our feelings are not there
to be cast out or conquered.
They're there to be engaged
and expressed with
imagination and intelligence.

~ T.K. COLEMAN

STANDARD 1

Control Your Emotions

IT'S OK TO CRY SOMETIMES

One of the trickiest topics to discuss when exploring female behaviors in the workplace is emotion, so let's talk about it first. Women in the workplace can't avoid this topic, but neither can men. Being sensitive to our own feelings and those of others is a great strength as leaders and team members. But our emotions can get the best of us sometimes. I thought it fitting to hit this one straight on as the first Stiletto Standard.

Picture this scene. I'm in a room with my boss. And he's yelling at me. No, not just yelling. He's in a full-on rampage. This man would often say to me "with a different turn of events, I'd be working for you." I considered him a professional. He taught leadership classes and coached executives. But in this moment, he had lost control of his emotions.

This was not the first time he had lost control. And in those other moments, I had lost my control, and I had cried. I had decided that I wasn't going to cry in front of him anymore. I also wasn't going to yell. I did my research and I had a talk with myself.

"Okay Suzanne," I told myself. "You tell others that they always have a choice, so what do you choose when this happens again? Are you going to yell back, cry, walk out? Or are you going stay calm and collected?"

I prepared myself for the emotional situations that I knew would happen again and chose a response that helped me stay in control and empowered me. So I was ready when again I was in a situation when this experienced professional was screaming like a toddler having a meltdown.

Why was he acting like this? I hadn't stolen something from his wallet. I hadn't besmirched his reputation. I hadn't even lost a client. The source of his rage was that I simply disagreed with him about a decision he had made. It was risky to disagree. I knew that. But I thought I got paid for my opinion as a leader in the organization.

His reaction seemed irrational to me. In my mind, my comment was reasonable. So when he chose to fly into a rage, I chose, this time, not to engage, not to cry, and not to run away in fear. Just like I would do with my toddler, I let him wear himself out. And, in an unexpected way, it felt really good. Why? Because he did not get the reaction he expected. He sent his angry words toward me like daggers, but I didn't let them sink into me. I just let them fall on the floor.

He did not get the power over me or whatever he was seeking from his tirade. After a moment or two, he calmed down and said that he couldn't talk any more and that he was too upset. He was upset, not me. What a relief. I sincerely hope that I don't ever find myself in this situation again. But, this is an approach, or a choice, that I will forever keep in my back pocket for future use, if needed.

Many of our behaviors are a result of our beliefs about what emotions are good and bad and which ones we are 'allowed' to express. Who we are is centered on our values, the things that we feel, and the emotions that drive us. There is no crime in feeling. Feelings are very real and very good for helping us form an opinion or make a decision. Because our feelings are our own, no one gets the right to tell us what they should be. And no one gets the power to make us lose control. The standard, and the source of our confidence and strength, is knowing that we can manage what's happening in our heads and hearts by expressing our feelings appropriately and managing them effectively. So let me emphasize that it's very important that we learn to be ourselves and to wear our high heels (or flats or wedges, your choice) with a great sense of confidence and inner strength.

WHEN YOU DON'T WANT TO CRY

For many women, being in a highly emotional state can result in tears. A strong emotional reaction to a person or situation sometimes seems weak when we think we need to be composed and competent. If a topic is important to you, of course you are going to feel emotional. The goal is to avoid emotional reactions that are embarrassing to you or that make others uncomfortable. There is no long-lasting harm in shedding a tear or two. It shows that you are real, passionate, and vulnerable. Vulnerability is a key element of building trust in relationships. With our friends and family it's certainly ok. But, in the workplace, it's just not something you want to happen on a regular basis. Above all, never, never use tears, or harsh words to manipulate or create a theatrical moment. This tactic will backfire.

When I think back to that pivotal moment when I made my choice, it is only fair to take into account what my boss may have been feeling. I did, after all, disagree with him. There were others in the room when it happened and while I may have thought I was being diplomatic in expressing an opposing view, perhaps he felt attacked. Perhaps he was embarrassed and perhaps he may even have thought I was on the side of right and was too proud to admit it. Does any of this warrant a rampage? No. Does it help me appreciate his point of view and help me understand how I might approach him differently in the future? Sure.

When our values or our point-of-view or beliefs are challenged, when what we are asked to do or be a part of is incongruent with our view of what's right or important, it can elicit strong feelings. Learning how to recognize, process, and express these feelings is what matters. Had my boss been a different person, he might have cried, or even left the room. He also might have also chosen to ask questions and listen. His choice was to attack back. His feelings got the best of him. What a shame.

HERE ARE SOME COPING MECHANISMS THAT WILL HELP YOU HOLD BACK THE TEARS:

- **EXPRESS YOURSELF.**

  Sometimes crying comes from not having expressed your feelings at all, ever. They get pent up and we puke them out in a very unbecoming scene. Learn to have courageous conversations along the way so your emotions don't build up into judgment, hatred, or uncontrollable outbursts. You must not allow strong feelings, or your fear of falling apart, to prevent you from doing the work that needs to be done. And part of that work is expressing yourself to others.

- **CHANGE THE CONVERSATION.**

  When emotions start to take over, change the channel. Self-talk can be very helpful here. Use self-talk, but instead of telling yourself not to cry, tell yourself to focus on the details of the other person or the situation. Focus your energy and your thoughts on what is really happening. Listen, really listen to them. Listen to their tone and their words. Ask more questions to learn what they are truly trying to express. See if you can separate your feelings from the issue at hand. Focus on them not you. You can cry later. I recommend waiting until you are in the car or at least out of ear shot. Crying in restrooms sometimes means the echo will work against you.

- **CHANGE THE SCENE.**

  Excuse yourself from the situation. If you cannot be

constructive, if you cannot focus, if you are going to need a tissue, if you didn't wear the water-proof mascara, leave. Be polite and professional. While you're out of the room, get prepared to address the topic again. Examine why you got upset. Was it fear, exhaustion, stress, or lack of information? Deal with that issue, which is yours, not theirs, and then get back in the game. One tip about leaving a room: If it's a group of people, just tell the person next to you that you'll be right back and leave, no speech, no need to announce your departure. If it's a single person, put up the polite index finger and just say, "I'll be right back."

- **LET THEM GO.**
Don't get intimidated by anyone, man or woman, yelling at you. Keep in mind that when a person yells, they have lost control of their emotions and might as well be blubbering. Hold it together and give them a chance to simmer down. At this point it's their problem, not yours. If it gets insulting or personal, don't fuel their fire. End the discussion professionally. If you feel physically threatened, leave immediately. Chances are, if they have a conscience, they will be embarrassed after all is said and done and you'll be able to work it out.

Crying is not the only way that we let go of emotional control. I'm not much of crier, except when an HGTV makeover is particularly moving or when the winner of The Voice is announced. My tendency is to use sarcasm and humor to avoid addressing the real issue. But the same standards apply to me when my emotions get out of control. Cracking a joke or insulting someone is not constructive. And the same standard applies to you, no matter what your emotional responses may be.

STANDARD STRATEGY

To explore this standard further, take a few minutes to answer the following questions for yourself. Then spend at least five minutes strategizing about situations that may arise in the next three months where you can apply this standard.

- *What do you do when your feelings are getting the best of you? Do you clam up, are you a screamer, or do you deploy passive aggressive tactics? Do you avoid situations that bring up raw emotions?*

- *Have you ever used tears to get ahead? Has it worked? What would you do differently next time?*

- *Do you feel you have to be perfect and not lose it in order to be great at what you do?*

YOUR TURN

What are your tactics for managing your emotions in stressful professional situations? Visit my Facebook page ***https://fb.me/SuzannesStandards*** and share your tactics!

LEARN MORE

It may seem that crying just makes our lives harder. But our tears serve more than one purpose. Only humans cry tears from emotion, either happy or sad, so at least when you cry, you know you're not a robot.

But research shows that our moods are often elevated after a good cry. Crying can be a form of catharsis that helps us release strong emotions, and feel more positive when we are done.

There's also evidence that the physical act of shedding tears helps release stress hormones from our brains and bodies.

Maybe it's time to change the assumptions people make about tears. Maybe our job is to help the non-criers get in touch with their humanity. And maybe it's time to worry a little less about if we cried and focus more on what we plan to do now that we're done crying and ready to get back to work.

READ MORE ABOUT CRYING AT
https://www.psychologytoday.com/blog/psych-unseen/201804/why-do-we-cry-exploring-the-psychology-emotional-tears

Her Story

I worked in a large organization where part of my job was to render expert opinion and advice to other members of the organization. I had given an expert advice to one member, Mary, who wanted to do a particular task her own way and didn't agree with my advice. My well-researched opinion stated that doing that task the way Mary wanted to do it would place the organization at financial risk.

Mary complained to a higher member of the organization, John. John called a meeting with both of us in order to resolve the issue, or so I thought. At the meeting John asked me pointed questions. He quickly became agitated and made derogatory remarks and accused me of not doing my job. At first, I defended my advice by providing concrete basis. Instead of listening, John became more agitated and his voice escalated. I soon realized he had committed himself to siding with Mary for reasons unbeknownst to me. He had to show Mary that he had her back.

I realized that this situation was beyond my control and I knew then that there was nothing I could say to change John's position. As I felt my blood pressure rise, I decided that I wasn't going to allow myself to be belittled. I was not going to engage in a shouting match, and I wasn't going to try to change his mind. Instead, I became silent for one minute, then said in a very low and controlled voice, that I will not be spoken to that way and left the room. He later apologized, in private, of course.

I believe that even when you are right and even when you feel justified in responding, removing yourself from any situation that is hurtful or belittling is always okay.

LOURDES SÁNCHEZ RIDGE, ESQUIRE
Pietragallo Gordon Alfano Bosick & Raspanti, LLP

NOTES

All you need is deep within you waiting to unfold and reveal itself. All you have to do is be still and take time to seek what is within, and you will surely find it.

~ EILEEN CADDY

STANDARD 2

Know Your Strengths

IDENTIFY, ARTICULATE, AND APPLY YOUR STRENGTHS

It was so generous of Mrs. Burns, my first grade teacher, to mark "talks too much" on the back of my report card. She pointed out to me, my parents, and on some occasions, the rest of the class that this girl liked to talk.

At first, I was embarrassed.

But as I thought it about it, I saw Mrs. Burns' checkmark and constant reminders about my loquaciousness as a sign. I like to talk to people. It comes naturally to me and I'm good at it. Therefore it must be something I'm supposed to do. So, from the first grade on, it's been official. I have great communication skills. And I have harvested great rewards and satisfaction from my innate gift of gab.

I've now had many years to discover other things that I do well and those I don't. Through self-assessment, missteps, successes, education, and feedback I have learned much about my capabilities. During the process I became a true believer in the power of applying our strengths.

In a collection of books, including *First, Break all the Rules* and *Now, Discover Your Strengths*, by Marcus Buckingham, presents us with an explanation of the strengths movement. Tom Rath and The Gallup Organization even offer us an opportunity to identify our strengths in an assessment found in *StrengthsFinder 2.0.* The overriding premise of the strength movement is that we stand to gain so much more from life and have the opportunity to give so much more to others if we identify, articulate, and apply our strengths. This strengths and abundance mentality movement is fueled by some of the greats like Donald O. Clifton, Peter Drucker, David Cooperrider, and Dr. Martin Seligman. These thinkers argue that if we (and the organization we work with) tap in to what we naturally do well, we will stay more motivated, generate more energy, and experience greater capacity for growth and excellence.

IDENTIFY YOUR STRENGTHS

What is a strength? A strength is a skill or competency that you are not only good at executing, but also experience joy in doing. It's something that brings out the authentic you. It's something you were meant to do. What topics are you drawn to most often? Which topics are you always curious to learn more about and explore? Those may be the topics and fields that would best utilize your strengths. Additionally, the activities you engage in that bring you energy are the ones that are tapping into your natural strengths. Be open to these signs and clues, because they will guide you toward your authenticity. Following these clues is the most important thing you can do to not only define what success means to you, but ultimately to experience it.

Should we ignore our weaknesses? Absolutely not. We have to know the areas where we are most likely to struggle or fail in order to manage our efforts around them. We can and should learn new skills along the way to stretch our minds and build on our capacity to contribute, but not at the expense of our strengths.

We have learned from leadership research that any strength, when overused, becomes a weakness. The feedback from Mrs. Burns, while corrective in nature, turned out to be a very helpful reminder to temper my natural strength. I needed to apply it effectively, but not hide it.

DEVELOP YOUR STRENGTHS

So, is it as easy as naming your strength and then voilà! - it's yours to claim and you can now capitalize on its value for evermore? Nope. You now need to invest and re-invest in that strength. Find the nuances that work for you. What more can you do to learn and develop it? How can you make sure others rely on you for it and know it is your strength?

Let's take the example of my communication skills for a spin. I identified this desire to communicate early on, but that didn't make me an expert at it. At the time, I was only active at it. It led me, however, to leadership roles in school and to the pursuit of a communications degree. I practiced public speaking, learned about communication theory, and I studied the dynamics of team and group communication. Throughout my career, I continued to hone my craft by taking more classes to focus my work on leadership and company culture. I amassed several certifications and relevant experiences to build my strength into a true area of expertise. Think about how this can work for other topics, like going from liking math to becoming a CFO; or from an attraction to logic, to building a career in supply chain management. I talked with a friend recently who is considering a career change. We talked about her strengths and she can now envision taking her skill of building a strong network of friends and colleagues and turning it into a lucrative sales career.

ARTICULATE YOUR STRENGTHS

Many women tend to shy away from speaking up about our successes. But what good is a strength if no one knows about it? How can you do your best work if your boss, your co-workers, or your subordinates are not aware of what your best contributions are or could be? In Peggy Klaus' book, *Brag! The Art of Tooting your Own Horn Without Blowing It*, she gives some great suggestions for informing others of what you have done well and in what areas you excel. Her advice is helpful if you are trying to get a promotion, sell a service, or simply get recognized as a stronger contributor on a team.

Sometimes, we believe that people should just recognize our good work without us speaking up. We think people should notice. But people are busy and are focused on their own situations and struggles. Too often we fail to express what we have done to make something a success. We diminish our role by sharing the credit with others or worse yet, we let someone else have it all. So, why not get good at connecting the dot for others? Show yourself and show others how your input and efforts impacted the final results.

APPLY ALL YOUR STRENGTHS

Strengths are like a team of draft horses. They are beautiful and strong when standing alone, and even more powerful when harnessed together as a team and put to work. Your gifts are unique. When they are connected together, they will unearth more opportunities and a greater sense of satisfaction than when working independently. It's your career, it's your happiness, it's your sense of accomplishment. So use your natural talents to get what you want. Be creative in finding opportunities at work and home, alone or with others, to practice strength-building exercises.

STANDARD STRATEGY

Here are five exercises that will help you to harvest the benefits of the strengths movement:

1. *Take some time to consider what you do well and what you really like to do. Reflect on what you have accomplished in your life. I suggest you keep a running list. How else will anyone know what to include in your retirement toast or eulogy? Look for the strengths that you applied in each situation. What opportunities do you have right now to talk about them or apply them? What steps will you take in the coming week to make your strengths work for you?*

2. *Think about a task or a project at work that you are avoiding. Chances are, you have put it off because it relates to one of your weaknesses. To complete it you will have to use a skill that does not fit the definition of a strength. You might have the skill, but get no satisfaction from doing it. Can you look at it differently? Can you tap into one of your strengths to help get it done? Is there someone you can include in the process whose strengths would make it easier or better?*

3. *Seek strength-building opportunities. Want to build on your love of_____? Fill in the blank with something like numbers, music, people, politics, leadership, public speaking, painting, problem solving. Volunteer, take a leadership role in a community organization, subscribe to a new publication, start your own blog, teach a class. These are all safe ways to explore, work, test and validate your strengths.*

4. *Seeing strengths in others is a great way to learn to recognize them in you. Tell someone what you appreciate about them; tell someone what you count on them for or what you find amazing about them. They will appreciate it and you may get some feedback of your own in return.*

5. *Buy* StrengthsFinder 2.0 *by Tom Rath, visit the website and take the online assessment using the code provided in his book. Upon completion of the online assessment you will be provided with a report that outlines and defines your five core strengths. The assessment helped me to see where I get my energy in life. It also helped me understand why I struggled when my strengths were not put to use. I often refer back to the report when I need a little reminder of the best ways to focus and plan.*

YOUR TURN

In my example of discovering a strength from Mrs. Burns, it was actually negative feedback that led me to the discovery of my strength. Have you ever had someone try to squash your strength, or fail to see how it could be put to good use? If so, what did you do?

Share with me how you discovered your strengths. Visit my Facebook page **https://fb.me/SuzannesStandards** and let me know!

LEARN MORE

Does your organization allow employees to use their strengths every day? If not, you as a leader, and your company, may be missing out on the best they have to offer. Here are six ways to create a culture that not only permits people to use their strengths but encourages it:

1. *Align organizational values around positive, growth-minded principles.*
2. *Hire, reward, and promote people who embrace and demonstrate company values.*
3. *Make sure leaders know their own strengths and limitations.*
4. *Create a performance management system that acknowledges and rewards strengths.*
5. *Work to define a clear purpose for people's strengths.*

6. *Provide expert strength coaches and support for professional development.*

According to Gallup analysis, people who use their strengths are "six times more likely to be engaged at work, 8% more productive and 15% less likely to quit their jobs." So why not work with their strengths?

READ MORE ABOUT USING STRENGTHS AT
http://news.gallup.com/businessjournal/186044/employees-strengths-outperform-don.aspx

Her Story

As a Strengths Coach, I help others gain awareness and appreciation of their strengths and how to apply them every day. It is an exciting journey that truly enhances their personal engagement and quality of life. My own journey began with recognizing my own God-given talents and how I can add knowledge and experience to them to create success and harmony in my professional and personal life. I have learned to seek out complementary partnerships when I find myself lacking in a needed talent; in my field that has been analytical thinking. My adaptability and activator strengths have empowered me to enjoy a joyful and varied career, realizing that I make things happen but can also take things as they happen. As a reminder, I have a piece of art in my office that defines what happiness is for me: when my work and words are of benefit to myself and others.

BARBARA STELLUTO
Certified strengths coach and organization development leader

NOTES

··

A woman is like a tea bag – you can't tell how strong she is until you put her in hot water.

~ ELEANOR ROOSEVELT

··

STANDARD 3

Sharpen Your Negotiation Skills

GET IN THE GAME

My dad only lectured me once as a teenager. OK, maybe there was only one lecture that stuck. It was brief, and to the point. He told me, "You will take responsibility for your own actions."

At 16, I don't think I understood the full impact of his words. I can tell you that I made better choices about staying out too late or doing something bad because I just wasn't sure what taking responsibility meant. Would he not pick me up at the police station? Would he leave me at the curb if I wrecked the car? I decided that I just didn't want to find out.

His words made negotiating with my inner bad girl and my friends about late night and weekend activities very easy. Dad would say that he was using what every good parent should use to keep their kids in line: fear. I would say that he prompted me to focus on a clear end result that I was able to negotiate into reality. This concept has worked in many aspects of my life.

To me, negotiating is all about taking responsibility for what happens in most any situation in your life. With the right skills and game plan, you will be free of the victim mentality. Whether you are negotiating bedtimes with kids, salaries with subordinates, or lease options on your car, you have some input and some control of the end results.

We face opportunities to negotiate all the time. Some of us relish the idea and go to battle with little thought or hesitation. Some of us simply recoil at the notion. Many equate negotiations with conflict, and conflict is something to avoid. Regardless of what goes through your mind, to maintain your edge in today's world, you must build strong, savvy negotiation skills.

Do we have to negotiate everything? No. Someone told us along the way to pick our battles. So pick 'em. If it's not something worth fighting for, something you are unwilling to change, then don't. But you have to accept the end result. There is nothing more empowering than embracing the fact that you always have a choice.

There are most certainly times when we have to engage. There are even times when we have to initiate a change or lay out a new deal on our own behalf. Let me tell you this: you will never get what you don't ask for. It's that simple.

I, like many women, err on the side of believing that the first offer, the first price, or the first solution is put out there with only my best interests in mind. I believe that people will give me the best deal possible the first time I ask.

Unfortunately, that's just not the case.

It's a very hard lesson for the optimists among us to accept. This does not mean that you will find me haggling with the sales clerk in Barnes and Noble over the price of a book or challenging a vendor on the prices of every service. It does mean, however, that in situations where the outcome is important to me, my team, or my family, I make sure that I explore possibilities to find what works best for everyone, including me.

Remember, people will follow their own form of logic when negotiating, not yours. They will not likely stick with your notions of what is fair. Even when you are thinking about someone else's needs, or trying to walk in their shoes, your thoughts are skewed by your own filters and experiences. Do approach every negotiating opportunity with the belief that what you want is possible and with the assumption that the other person has good intentions, even though their intentions might not meet your needs.

■■■

Stand up straight and realize who you are, that you tower over your circumstances.

~ MAYA ANGELOU

■■■

TIME TO NEGOTIATE

To be sure you are poised to walk away on those stilettos a winner, use these tips:

- **STIR UP CREATIVE SOLUTIONS.**

  If you really want something that you believe the other person will find incredibly outrageous, present it like this. "Just for fun, let's explore something extreme, what if I said that I wanted ___X___?" Then, sit back and watch and wait. Your idea may not be as far off as you originally thought. They may see something positive in your suggestion that you didn't see. If they freak out, well, you know where you stand and you can now explore their objections and create other possibilities together.

- **USE YOUR WOMANLY WILES.**

  What's a wile? Here's what I say: wiles are gifts that women have such as intuition, empathy, and sensitivity. While these feminine gifts should never be used for deceit or ill-gotten gains, they do give us an advantage. Pay careful attention to how someone is reacting to you. Use your wiles, not only to understand the other person, but to persuade them to your point of view. Intimidation tactics and anger are not required elements for good negotiating. Neither are flirting or diminishing your self-worth. Many a great deal has been made through the more noble powers of trust, sincerity and compassion.

- **EMBRACE THE POWER OF CHOICE.**

  Saying no is an option, really! It's not just saved for the sales guy on the showroom floor or for a female colleague

*on the other side of the table. It's a choice you have, too.
You can also choose to think about it. Save the next part
of the discussion for another day. The best deals are built
over time. Don't let the impulse buyer in you force you to
agree to something that won't make you happy in the
long run.*

- **PREPARE YOURSELF FOR BATTLE.**
  *If you expect to be taken seriously, then take what you
  need to do seriously. You have chosen to engage in the
  battle, now prepare yourself for victory. Victory is not
  always about winning, it is about getting a result that
  works for you and, in the best of scenarios, leaves the
  other party satisfied as well.*

  HOW TO GET PREPARED:

  1. *Define the situation and the results that you want.
     Be very clear about what you want out of the
     conversation before you go in. Build a solid case
     around your position. What possible variations
     exist within your proposal that would allow for
     compromise? What elements in your idea shows a
     willingness to collaborate? When do you draw the
     line? When do you say no?*

  2. *Acknowledge what the other person might feel or
     believe about the situation and be ready to affirm
     them or educate them. The best way to affirm
     someone is to engage in what I call positive
     listening. Nod your head yes to show that you
     understand what the other person is saying.*

Comprehension is not agreement, but it goes a long way toward building mutual respect. People don't always want to be right, but they do always want to be heard and understood.

3. *Develop a strategy for getting the negotiation started. Presenting an ultimatum at the onset is best only in very rare situations. You could start with a "what if" question, a story, a recent study, or a candid comment. What will make it most comfortable for your adversary? Watch your timing as well. Schedule the conversation for when they are mostly likely to be in a positive state. You want them relaxed and open to ideas, not put on guard.*

4. *Imagine the worst-case scenarios. Use what you know about the person and their behavior in prior situations to predict possible outcomes. How could you react to each scenario to keep the conversation going in a productive manner? Prepare possible answers to give or questions to ask. If you get caught off-guard, be silent and let them work through their own thoughts as you work through yours. Then re-start the conversation in a calm, constructive manner.*

5. *Identify what you can give back or give up. Sometimes people just want to feel that they didn't give away everything. Preserving someone's ego or reputation by working with them on how the*

outcome is communicated is very powerful. Giving up something that means little to you, but shows your willingness to compromise, can make it easier for them to give you what's important to you in return.

ONE FINAL TIP: The toughest negotiator you will ever encounter is the voice in your head. So, build your case, prepare yourself and get out of your own way.

STANDARD STRATEGY

Think about a positive negotiating experience that you have had. What went well and why? Do the same for one that went poorly. Make note of what you learned from each scenario.

If you typically recoil at the thought of negotiating, find opportunities to practice your negotiation savvy in small ways and build your confidence from there. What are they?

If you tend to charge right into any negotiating opportunity, analyze your results. Are you getting long-term, meaningful results? If not, try tapering your approach by creating a strategy before diving in.

WANT TO LEARN MORE?

I highly recommend Ching-Ning Chu's book *The Art of War for Women* based on Sun Tzu's ancient strategies for winning wars. It provides great ideas and perspectives for negotiation.

YOUR TURN

Negotiation is the one thing that I can think of, other than drinking tequila, which tends to elicit immediate fear in women, but brings out the bravado in men.

Do you think men are naturally better negotiators? Share your thoughts about negotiation at *https://fb.me/SuzannesStandards.*

LEARN MORE

You have probably heard of the phrase "body language." It's when we, intentionally or unintentionally, share messages with other people without using words.

But, did you know that more than half of all communication is non-verbal? Some research would tell us it's a much as 70%. That means the way we position our bodies, whether we make eye-contact, our facial expressions, and even nodding - or not nodding - our heads are saying something. All of these movements convey subtle signals to other people. Sometimes the signals match our words, sometimes they don't.

And sometimes, misunderstandings and problems can result by not understanding non-verbal communication. There are cultural differences in non-verbal communications, but even men and women mean different things with their body language.

One of the biggest differences in non-verbal communication is nodding. In a conversation or negotiation, men usually nod to indicate agreement. Women will often nod to indicate they understand what you are saying, but their nod doesn't necessarily mean that they agree.

You can just imagine how in a negotiation, a nod from a woman might be misunderstood by a man. He might think she's accepted his low-ball offer. Or the failure of a man to nod might make the woman think he can't grasp the difficult concept she's trying to share.

Of course there are differences in individuals. And there are many other aspects of non-verbal communication to learn. But now you know one place to start.

READ MORE ABOUT BODY LANGUAGE AT
https://online.pointpark.edu/public-relations-and-advertising/gender-differences-communication-styles/
Learn even more about the power of your presence in Amy Cuddy's research-based book, *Presence*

Her Story

Working in construction as the leader of a woman-owned business can be challenging. There are times that not only do you have to prove you are capable, but that you are intelligent enough to solve an issue without asking your male staff members for assistance. I try to live by the motto that I don't need to hit you over the head with my experience or knowledge; over time you will realize by my work product that I have it.

We were on a large project and our crew fell behind in accomplishing our work. It was determined that crews from another company would need to be brought in at my company's expense to help complete the work. I understood the reason for the decision, but I was upset that the additional crew's expenses were being charged to my company for over three times the rate of the industry standard. I called the company supplying the additional crews and they refused to alter their numbers. I notified the contractor we were working for and they were only interested in using the rates that were submitted.

Needless to say I was extremely angry. I decided to wait and calm down. I knew I would not accomplish anything in the state I was in. Approximately six months later, after the other company was paid in full by the contractor, I went to the contractor whom we were still working for. I asked for a meeting with the key decision maker. I knew I needed to ask for what I thought was fair. At that meeting I presented my rationale. The contractor listened and to my surprise agreed to my request a day later. There were some conditions attached to the agreement, but in the long run the conditions were under my control and I agreed.

I would always encourage you to ask for what you want, in my case, time made all the difference. The end result was not all that I wanted but it was much better than not asking at all.

PATRICIA CHILDS THORNHAM
President, Advance Terrazzo Co.

NOTES

Change is hard at first,
messy in the middle and gorgeous
at the end.

~ ROBIN SHARMA

STANDARD 4

Learn To Make Change

IT HAPPENS, WHETHER YOU LIKE IT OR NOT

As an adult, yes, you should be able to handle making change for a $15.49 purchase when handed a $20.00 bill, but I'm talking about something else here.

Change happens. Shifts happen. Sometimes we instigate it, sometimes we fight it. To be the polished professional or graceful matriarch that we hope to be, we have to get really good at dealing with it.

Sometimes we're the ones pushing for change. It can be hard when we are eager and hopeful but others are negative and resistant. Have you ever spent a productive Saturday afternoon re-arranging the living room furniture only to have your family come home and cry, "What did you do that for?" That feels good doesn't it?

Sometimes we're the ones who have to deal with an un-expected change. We can't stop the change, so we grouch and whine about it. Have you ever spent a lunch break complaining about the latest stupid idea that management has come up with, or the new process for kids drop off and pick up? Can't get that hour of fruitless conversation back now, can you?

Sometimes, we pretend to accept a change but all the while we are sneaking around, trying to sabotage the new system.

Raise your hand if you've ever nodded yes to the new-fangled process for doing your work only to go back to the old way when no one is looking? Tsk, tsk, tsk.

It's fundamentally hard to get people to change. I'm sure you have experienced it. Did you really believe that your kids were going to quickly embrace the new family rules that you've so painstakingly created from a Pinterest-inspired design? You've posted it on the fridge hoping everyone would take the hints and immediately get along better, pick up their socks or load the dishwasher? That's ok, so did I.

Chances are you've been in on good and bad change efforts, whether you are trying to make it happen or if it's happening to you.

When it comes to their relationship with change, people sit somewhere on a spectrum that ranges from disdain to love. Regardless of where you live on the spectrum, you can be sure that people around you represent the full range of reactions to change. There are those who fight change at every turn. Let's call them the Rocks of Gibraltar. Then there are those who seek and embrace it at every turn. We can call them the Ever-Readies. Ever-Readies might get up in the morning and move the living room furniture. Rocks spend a great effort getting that furniture the way they want it and won't ever move a thing. Ever.

BARRIERS TO CHANGE

Whether you want to make something better or dare to try something new, things will get in the way. It's important to recognize these barriers in yourself and others before and during times of change. Take a look at a couple of barriers that I have identified below. As you read about them, consider how you have reacted to change in the past. Also think about how others (the change lovers, the change haters, and those living somewhere in between) might react.

First, let's pretend that you are the manager of a customer service group. You need to change the day or time of the weekly staff meeting because the current arrangement is conflicting with a personal commitment. Because it's a call center, meetings have to be before or after regular business hours.

Now, consider the following barriers to change. Which one sounds most like you and can you recognize the opportunity you have to do better?

FEAR

As the manager you might argue that you have the right to simply make the announcement. Ok, you do, but is that going to be very effective and motivating? Probably not. Some employees might have a fear of a bus schedule going bad, a babysitter not cooperating, or other legitimate concerns about how a new schedule will impact their daily lives.

The unknown is scarier for some people more than others. To minimize fear, get or disclose as many specifics about the change as you can. Don't be critical of fear. Find ways to address it. The fears may not be rational, but they feel real.

It can also help to give a sound reason for the change. If you give no reason for the change, people have a hard time accepting it or trusting your judgement.

Giving people time to prepare is another way to minimize fear. You might announce the new date or time a few weeks in advance to allow everyone to accept the idea and to adjust their own personal commitments.

MISTRUST

Sometimes people resist change because they have had a bad experience in the past. So ask yourself, what's your history with change? What's the other person's history with change? If previous experience has been negative, then trust might be an issue for anyone involved. Even if there is no history, there can be a lack of trust. When there is little or no trust on anyone's part, change can be difficult.

If you're an employee in the above scenario and you don't trust your manager, you might have a lot of doubts. You might wonder if the meeting times will keep changing. You might wonder if the manager is changing days and times just to mess with you. These uncertainties need to be worked out. How have schedule changes been made before? If this is the first time, it might be best to let it be. Assume the manager's personal reasons for the change are valid and move on. But if the changes keep happening, brainstorm what positive suggestions you could offer to help address the issue. Ask your manager if this will be a rotating schedule. Offer solutions rather than complaints, because complaining helps no one.

LOSS OF CONTROL

Adults don't like to be told what to do. As children, we don't have a lot of control over our lives. We're told when to go to school, when to be home, what to wear, even when to go to bed. But we've made it to adulthood, and now we want to make our own choices, thank you very much. Being very direct when giving work instructions or in an emergency is ok, but if you try to control too much about other people during times of change, things will backfire.

When you are the manager making the scheduling change, you have the option of transferring some control to your staff. By reducing any feeling about being a victim or losing control, you can make the change easier and more successful. Giving your staff some control can help them buy-in to the change more readily. Asking for their input helps them feel like they have a say in the solution. Let them work out some options or even make the final decision.

LAZINESS

People get very comfortable with routine. Change feels like too much work for many people. They can appear very lazy.

As either the manager or employee in our scenario, you have the responsibility to bring the too-comfortable ones out of their current state and into the new one. You will be a shining star if you can influence others around you to embrace new ideas and opportunities. If you are the lazy one, grab a hold of an Ever-Ready colleague who, as an early-adopter of change, will energize you and others into action. Let their energy and perspective inspire you.

If you are an Ever-Ready changer, like me, be very careful that you are making changes for the best reasons. Don't make them out of panic, boredom or your adult onset A.D.D. It is very frustrating for employees or family members to have to follow you if you randomly make adjustments and improvements. I have followed a boss who loved to change and have gotten dizzy from running in circles trying to keep up with her every new idea. Practice patience with others. People do what makes sense to them and if changing doesn't look, feel or seem right, they may need more time and more information. Provide an atmosphere that supports their needs too. Giving others time and information will get them committed to the change, which is much better than compliance.

Incredible change happens in your life when you decide to take control of what you do have power over instead of craving control over what you don't

~STEVE MARABOLI

STANDARD STRATEGY

Change can sometimes be risky. In our world, change often occurs so rapidly it's downright scary. What kind of change scares you?

- *What are your personal obstacles to handling change?*

- *What changes have you successfully implemented? Did you have to bring others along? What worked for you, and what didn't work?*

YOUR TURN

Have you encountered an obstacle to change not covered here? Share it with me on my website at **https://fb.me/SuzannesStandards.** Let me and others know how you handled it.

LEARN MORE

Think of the last time you were startled. How did you react? Did you try to run away? Or did you turn around and confront the danger?

How we handle startling or frightening situations is usually controlled by a part of our brains called the limbic system. The limbic system controls really basic emotions like fear, pleasure, and anger. This part of our brain is all about instinct and when humans experience a threat, the limbic system triggers our fight-or-flight response.

Being confronted with change in the workplace can often turn on that fight-or-flight response. For many people, a simple schedule change, or location change, can be seen as a threat. Emotional changes can engage the limbic system, too.

For some, their instinct is to fight. This shows up as aggression or confrontation. For others, their instinct is to take flight, or flee. That could result in checking out of work and not completing tasks.

People may not even realize how much their limbic system influences their reactions. But now that you know, you can try to minimize relying on only the fight-or-flight response when you face change. You can also work to make the workplace a secure environment and reduce emotional and physical threats. Then the limbic system takes a break and the more logical, rational parts of the brain take over.

READ MORE ABOUT THE LIMBIC SYSTEM
https://donrheem.com/you-brains-limbic-system-roadmap-to-productivity/

Her Story

I love new beginnings. When I think of changes I've experienced in my life, I tend to reflect back on career transitions, and I've had quite a few. The blessings of each transition is the opportunity to bring the best of me forward to my new job for good and the opportunity to learn and grow in a new way or different direction. I admit that I naturally sit closer to the Ever-Ready end of the change continuum and often seek change as way to get re-energized and excited about something new. I have not always been this way, but recognize that my comfort with change and my tolerance for risk increased with each transition. In my career I have worked with many leaders and organizations during times of change. I have found, and research supports, that the loss of control is the biggest barrier. So, if you are facing a change or transition, get control by embracing the change and find within it what you can learn and how you can grow. Use the change to bring out the best in you.

LESLIE BONNER
Owner, Bonner Consulting

NOTES

Style is the packaging for a product; your substance is the product

~ CHIN-NING CHU

STANDARD 5

Manage Your Brand

BE MEMORABLE FOR ALL THE
RIGHT REASONS

What do you think of when you hear big brand names like Apple, Coca Cola or Target? Companies work hard and invest significant money to build brands with a certain vibe, feeling, or quality that people associate with them.

You may think only corporations have a brand, but surprise! You have a brand, too. When a company begins the journey of establishing its brand, the goal is to get you and me (or whomever they seek to spend money on their products) to take notice and react positively. Do you want the same thing?

Consider what people think, suppose, or assume when they see you. Perception does depend on the viewer, true. But ask yourself if you have done a good job of creating the image of yourself that elicits the responses you want. Does your outside represent what's inside?

As a young girl, I created a very clear picture of the woman that I wanted to be when I grew up. It was a compilation of traits held by women I admired combined with expectations others had of me. So often we think of ourselves as perceived through the eyes of others. It would be wonderful if we could start with the vision of how we want to see our own self from the inside. Even when we mature and can appreciate who we have become, we still have to manage the world's view of us to build trust, develop partnerships, attract clients, teach others, and more. It takes work and inspiration.

When I was a senior in high school, my mother gave me a book as a Christmas present. It was Helen Gurley Brown's, *Having it All*. Mom recognized that the vision of who I wanted to be when I grew up might come to fruition with a little help from the editor-in-chief of Cosmopolitan magazine. She was right. This book inspired me at age 17. I read it again recently as an adult and even though it has lost much of its relevance, there were still helpful sections. No, not the detailed bits of advice on sex that my mother probably didn't know were in there. I'm talking about the three key areas to consider when managing the world's view of you.

The only time you should look down on a women is to compliment her shoes.

~UNKNOWN

APPEARANCE

The first and most obvious is your appearance. If you don't have respect for how you look, you can't expect others to respect you. Showing respect for yourself will garner respect from others. You don't have to be a style guru. Think of women you most admire that live a similar lifestyle as you. What do they wear? What can you do to develop a wardrobe and style that makes you feel good on the inside fuels your confidence?

Here are some timeless tips, some collected from Helen Gurley Brown and some that I picked up along the way.

- *Invest in clothes on purpose. Don't love something just because it's in style or on sale. Decide what works for you then buy pieces that bring you joy and support your brand. Take your time and avoid wasting your hard-earned money on clothes that don't serve you.*

- *Accessories can update an outfit and give a little flair. They are often great conversation starters. Choose wisely and be willing to edit your look before you walk out the door. Consider investing in some timeless classics like diamond studs, pearls and a good watch to have on hand when the occasion calls for a conservative look.*

- *Dress for the occasion. Think about how your outfit will enable you to connect most comfortably to others in situations that matter. (Some may argue that all situations matter). Wearing your yoga ensemble to seek funding for anything other than a health-related cause, for example, will make you comfortable, but might not impress your investors.*

- *Keep your shoes, stilettos or not, in good repair and on your damn feet. You bought them, you wear them until the end of the dance! Again, you may not see the need, but others do.*

- *Keep your nails clean, uniform in length and maintain your polish. Don't let the remnant of last month's gel mani distract someone during an important conversation.*

- *Choose a hair stylist that will help you look like you are paying attention to current trends and gives you a cut that you can manage. If you can't style it yourself or afford someone to do daily for you, try something else.*

- *Wear foundational garments (this means underwear) that fit and do what they are designed to do, or why bother. Don't give anyone you encounter any reason to be distracted by your malfunctioning bra or underwear that rides up. Give them every reason to look you straight in the eyes.*

- *Perfume is for your pleasure, your comfort, not everyone else's in the room. Keep it subtle, sister.*

BEHAVIOR AND ATTITUDE

Branding goes well beyond outward appearances. It is also created through your disposition and behaviors. Attitude is the second key element to a strong personal brand and it is the best tool for overcoming a bad hair day or an unfortunate outfit choice. Companies like Nike, Walmart, and Serta want you to feel something when you see their logos or ads. They have every intention of stirring up a particular emotional response. Whether it's drive, familiarity or peacefulness, they carefully select words, music and images to reinforce that feeling. What kind of emotions do you bring out in others? Your attitude has a very strong effect on the people around you. It speaks volumes in an instant. Keeping and displaying a healthy, positive attitude in all situations helps everyone.

CONSIDER THESE IDEAS:

Walk around with a smile on your face. People may wonder what you've been up to or what secret you hold, but you will look like someone they want to talk to.

If someone speaks to you or even gives you a friendly smile speak or smile back, even if you don't know them. What a wonderfully positive and inexpensive gift to give.

- *Show respect for others, including their space, their time, and their opinions.*
- *Keep the gossip to a dull roar. It may feel good, but it certainly doesn't make anyone look good, most specifically, you.*
- *You are not better than anyone else. Don't act like it.*
- *You are not less than anyone else. Don't act like it.*
- *It's not all about you. Listen more than you talk, ask more than you tell and accept more than you deny.*
- *Shake hands firmly, no limp wrists. Be the first to initiate a handshake. Show confidence.*

APTITUDE

The third key element for developing a powerful brand is aptitude. If there is nothing behind the good clothes and positive attitude, you have a problem and people will know it. If Nike's shoes fall apart after one lap around the mall, if a Serta mattress goes flat in four months or Walmart's prices are not lower than other stores, all branding efforts become null and void. As women, we have to be able to demonstrate our substance. We have to show that we know what we are talking about. We need to have confidence in our ideas and be able to articulate our capabilities. We have to let others know that our actions and words back the image we present.

HOW DO YOU DEMONSTRATE APTITUDE?

Wait your turn then take your turn. We learned early on in life to be polite and take turns. Studies show that girls on elementary school playgrounds are expected to do it more than boys. It's ok to wait to speak, but when it is your turn, step up and do what you need to do. Hit the ball out of the park!

- **EXPRESS YOURSELF WITH CONFIDENCE.**
  Do your research, whether it's a PTA meeting or a board meeting, get your thoughts and ideas together. Think things through, prepare some strong sound bites that reflect your position or proposal with clarity.

- **BE CURIOUS. SEEK NEW PERSPECTIVES AND IDEAS.**
  You do not have to have all the answers. There is no

better way to show aptitude than to show that you have the capacity to grow and learn.

- **ACKNOWLEDGE THE CONTRIBUTIONS OF OTHERS.**
  You don't know it all; you need the input and ideas of everyone. Graciously accept what anyone has to offer. What you do with it is up to you.

STANDARD STRATEGY

Take a few minutes to picture 3 people you respect. List them here and try to put into words what you admire or like about them. From there, pick a few skills or behaviors that you can work on as you build your brand.

READ MORE

For further inspiration, I highly, highly recommend the book *Simple Abundance* by Sarah Ban Breathnach. This little gem will help you uncover that which makes you "you" and guide you toward creating the brand that is authentic and all yours.

YOUR TURN

Have you developed a signature brand? Visit *https://fb.me/SuzannesStandards* and tell me what it is that makes you distinctly you, and how you arrived at your brand.

LEARN MORE

Want to know the secret to feeling good inside and out? First, go on a brisk 10-minute walk.

Sweating a little? Breathing hard? You can thank me later. Your self-esteem should be on the rise right now thanks to the feel-good hormones pumping through your brain.

But the positive side effects of exercise aren't just a little mood boost. According to research, working out regularly, which means following a routine for at least six months can reduce anxiety and depression. It can also help boost your self-confidence.

Of course, I know we're all busy. And we'll talk about how to handle busy schedules in a few chapters. So it's also important to know that working out and exercising doesn't have to happen in hours-long sessions. In fact, you can take short breaks to get your heart rate up throughout the day and get the same benefits. So bring those walking shoes to work and stash a set of dumbbells under your desk. When you're on hold, do some squats. When you're heading to a meeting, take the stairs instead of the elevator.

Exercising and working out isn't just about your appearance. In fact, the internal changes in your self-esteem and confidence might be more important than changes in weight or inches. There's nothing more attractive than a person who feels strong and empowered. When you feel good, you are more effective and can create a fantastic personal brand.

LEARN MORE ABOUT THE BENEFITS OF EXERCISE HERE
https://www.elitedaily.com/p/how-working-out-makes-you-more-confident-from-the-inside-out-according-to-science-8565734

Her Story

Appearance was always important to me. When I moved to the USA from the Ukraine in 2008, it was hard to realize that not everyone cared about their looks. I think that the way you look is a reflection of how you treat other people. I feel your appearance is most important when you're at work.

As a hair stylist, I feel that my hair should always be presentable, because when I work with my clients I want them to feel comfortable. People will not take me seriously if I look like a mess and my hair looks bad. I believe my work is more than just about styling hair, we make people feel good about themselves and it's very satisfying. Even if you have a bad day, but you have to go to work, and if you put a little effort into looking presentable, you realize that you feel better and people treat you with respect. You don't have to spend a fortune on your clothes and make up, just wear the right clothes that fit your body. I also believe that the way you look makes you behave differently. When you're wearing sweatpants you manage to act more relaxed and don't think about your appearance compared to when you dress up, your attitude is different.

There are so many things that make you who you are. it is also dependent on what kind of people you are around and where you are. We all act different in different situations and with different people, for example we are one person with our children vs. coworkers and so, no matter who you are with, at that moment you should always act with integrity and show respect to others.

OLENA SAVTCHOUK
Certified Beauty Consultant, Philip Pelusi Salons

NOTES

My philosophy is that not only are you responsible for your life, but doing the best at this moment puts you in the best place for the next moment.

~OPRAH WINFREY

STANDARD 6

Develop & Practice Political Savvy

LEARN HOW THE GAME IS PLAYED

As a young, enthusiastic, and perhaps overzealous, professional, I started my first real career-building job. I had a lot of hope and optimism and I came out of the gate running. I found projects to do, discovered ways to make change, and identified people to get to know. Then one day, a new friend with years of experience at this organization pulled me aside.

"They will break you. Eventually you won't feel so optimistic and happy," she said.

What a downer!

"Gee, thanks," I said. "But they won't break me. No one gets to mess with my cheery disposition."

Five years later, I was broken. I felt beaten by the culture and the old boy political system. I negotiated myself out of there.

I hadn't failed at the job. I hadn't even done bad work. I had, in fact, produced good work that helped the organization. I met performance goals. I built relationships with everyone that I could.

But I had failed to read and respond effectively to the culture and the way things were done there. At the time, I felt like they did 'break' me. In hindsight, I realize I simply did not have the skills to play the game in a way that not only fueled my cheery disposition, but also protected me from falling prey to my own naiveté.

OFFICE POLITICS

Understanding a work culture and the office politics within it is a skill everyone needs but isn't typically taught in the accounting, communications, or information technology classes we take. Office politics refers to the unwritten rules, the ways things are really done, in a place of business. When you start work in a new organization you need to figure out the answers to these questions.

- *How are decisions made?*
- *What information is shared readily, and what isn't?*
- *How is the rumor grapevine fed and squashed?*
- *Is collaboration expected and rewarded?*
- *And what kind of behavior do you see from leadership and what will they tolerate?*

You need to know the political environment of your company or organization and play it well or it will play you. There is no shame, none, nada, in understanding and navigating through the political scene. The shame lies in letting it, or your disdain or avoidance of it, keep you down. In fact, if you don't learn the lay of the political landscape, you may suffer. You may get professionally or personally hurt by decisions, changes, or promotions that you just didn't see coming.

Understanding the underlying energy in an environment is not easy. We go through the day completing our work, but not paying attention to the clues around us. Do you look at who sits where during meetings? Who is always allowed to be late or skip meetings, and who is not? Who speaks up at meetings, and who stays silent? What is the stated dress code, and is it enforced? Is debate encouraged or squashed? Do new ideas evaporate in the air, or are they welcomed and explored?

The politically savvy among us read these cultural signs and use them to create opportunities or even to build protection from a highly political environment. Here is one simple clue that you can explore in your own organization. It may speak volumes about the political landscape.

When an email is sent to the entire office, examine the "To:" field. Are the "to" addresses in random, alphabetical, or hierarchical order?

If the email addresses are random, it usually signifies casualness and means that this company is not married to process or set norms. The norm may even be carelessness or lack of discipline. But even in chaos, there is order, so working in the environment requires a little trial and error to see what rules are important and decide how best to live within them.

If the email addresses are listed alphabetically, that can demonstrate fairness and an intentional show of equal respect. This is a company that means well and might have strong collaborative structure. You could assume that everyone has an equal opportunity to contribute. It may also mean that everything is so neat and tidy and everyone so polite and well-behaved that true innovation and creative problem solving is difficult.

If the email addresses are organized in hierarchical order with the important people first, lesser people last, this is a sign of a cultural that gives more power to titles. It's a status thing. Any one individual's ability to influence is in direct correlation with their place on the corporate ladder. This culture produces competition among its ranks, which can be good and bad, but you can at least understand the rules and go from there.

Your organization may use more progressive communication tools, online chat, websites, or other discussion channels. Use a similar lens to learn how things are really done. How ideas are shared, discussed and encouraged is a fantastic reflection of the culture norms and political climate of any organization.

Once you recognize that every environment has political undertones, learning the rules at your workplace will only help you on your way to a savvy status. The next step and key to positive political savvy is finding a way to fit in to the existing culture while speaking with your own voice and acting from your own beliefs.

Being politically savvy is not about compromising values. It's not about being less than honest or appearing disingenuous. Playing is not the same as being a player. Players are overt manipulators who use their political skill for nothing but personal gain. Players position themselves in a favorable light with leaders, often at the expense of others and the organization.

STICK TO THE POSITIVE

Being politically savvy means choosing how you will act within the culture. And your best move is to act in a positive way. Positive political behavior means using power and influence to advance the team and organizational interests.

- **BE INCLUSIVE.**

   Share information with everyone who has a vested interest in the project or topic. For some, withholding information is a power play and a way to control people and outcomes. It can backfire when people play the same secretive way.

- **DISALLOW NEGATIVE BEHAVIOR.**

   Don't pick fights with or embarrass a player. Do refuse to take their behavior personally. That's what they want. Instead, redirect their attempts at getting control of you or a project you're working on by sticking to discussions about problems, not personalities.

- **EQUALIZE POWER STATUS.**

   Make those on your staff feel equal, worthy, and empowered at all times. Never 'junior' somebody. It does not look pretty. You get more power by giving it to others.

AVOID THE NEGATIVE

How do you know if something strays into the realm of negative political behavior? The basic test question is, does this action use power and influence with malicious intent? Let's look at some examples.

- *Holding 'the meeting after the meeting'. Gathering to discuss or criticize what just occurred in a scheduled committee or team meeting can be negative. It's ok to seek more information from others and further explore issues, and even gauge buy-in for new ideas, but if the conversation should have happened during the meeting, it's not supportive of a healthy culture.*

- *Pumping people for information only to share it later. Be wary of the person who wants to know all that you are thinking and feeling. Unless this person is your coach or mentor, be discreet. Players have a knack for using personal information against others.*

- *Using power and influence to advance self-interest. Don't be the one whose arguments or opinions are always about your department or your feelings. Show that your efforts are in the best interest of the company.*

A political environment, just like our country's political system, is a complicated maze of personal motivation, altruistic intentions, and misguided manipulation. Be very purposeful about the part you play in your company's culture. Don't let the politics break you down, make you lose sight of your goals, or cause you to sacrifice your sense of right and wrong. Look for clues and find little ways, every day, to make a positive difference.

∎∎

I think the one lesson I have learned is that there is no substitute for paying attention.
~DIANE SAWYER

∎∎

STANDARD STRATEGY

Can you think of a time when you were a victim of political play? Rewind the scenario in your mind and look for clues that might have helped you along the way. Pay attention to how others reacted to you. What questions did people ask? What did they do or not do that might have helped? Can you see what you missed the first time? What could you have done differently?

Do you know someone at work who needs to be a little more aware of the politics around her? Is she missing cultural clues that you can see? What can you do to help?

YOUR TURN

Are there other examples of positive and negative political power plays that you have learned to handle? Or that you need help handling?

Visit **https://fb.me/SuzannesStandards** and let's discuss how to handle office politics.

LEARN MORE

We all love the players, but hate the game, especially in office politics, right? But what if I told you there was a way to understand that playing the game right can actually help you be a better, more successful employee? It can also help your co-workers be more successful, and overall benefit your organization?

Learning about game theory is an interesting way to tackle the inevitable political and power interactions at the office. We're familiar with games that have a winner and a loser, or multiple losers. That's called a zero-sum game. A win-win game is one where more than one player can win, especially if people work together. Sometimes compromise and sacrifice are involved.

Researchers have won Nobel prizes for studying which kind of game theory leads to the best results. And the answer is that when individuals work together for their own benefit and the benefit of the collective good.

Here's an example:

Employee 1 and Employee 2 are working on different parts of the same project. Employee 1 observes Employee 2 making a critical statistical mistake in their work. Employee 2 observes Employee 1 presenting his or her work in a way that is damaging to the company as a whole. Both employees have unknowingly made a mistake and both have two options:

1. *Do not confront the other employee with the mistake and report the mistake to management (Report).*
2. *Confront the other employee and help correct the mistake immediately (Confront). (This situation assumes all employees involved will not ignore a critical mistake.)*

Employee 1 and 2 both have two options each which creates four possible outcomes. Each employee has the ability to score between 0 and 5 (office) political points.

Outcome 1: Both employees choose option two and confront each other on their respective mistakes. The mistakes are corrected immediately and work output increases. Employee 1 receives a score of 4; Employee 2 receives a score of 4. This outcome produces the best overall result for all parties involved."

In order for this to work, everyone has to play by the same rules. It can be hard for people to transition from zero-sum to win-win. Many people just don't believe a win-win situation truly does benefit them. In that case, you need to work on building trust before you can get people to buy in to the win-win situation.

LEARN MORE ABOUT GAME THEORY AT
https://www.linkedin.com/pulse/applying-game-theory-workplace-chris-comer/

Her Story

I was about mid-career and hired as a Director of Staffing in a large, global pharmaceutical company. This was the first time in my life and career that I was working with scientists and engineers, having spent the first 10+ years in the consumer marketing world of banking and financial services.

The pharma culture was very "scientific," and required extensive data and facts to influence behavior, especially for an HR leader. I had received these "cultural signals" very early on in my tenure there – many times being asked to provide the "why" and not just the "how." I even had to brush up on the legal backdrop that drove such requirements as applicant tracking!

Imagine if I chose to believe that these people were acting this way just to play me, or to gain advantage. It was quite the opposite, in fact. Theses "scientific" minds were doing what they do best and this case, doing my best meant adapting to meet their needs.

I realized that to survive and thrive in this new world that I needed to understand how scientists think and are trained. Rather than be intimidated or think that I didn't fit there, I needed to live in the world of observations and data; to create hypotheses and proofs. As a result, I was more effective and able to work differently to navigate in a culture that was new to me. Frankly, this approach taught me to be a much better HR leader, regardless of the context.

TRACY GRAJEWSKI
President, Laurel Summit Insights

NOTES

··

*To be yourself in a world that
is constantly trying to make you
something else is the greatest
accomplishment.*

~RALPH WALDO EMERSON

··

STANDARD 7

Refine Your Leadership Style

BE AUTHENTIC TO BE EFFECTIVE

I attended a women-in-leadership workshop recently and was asked this very powerful question: "Who is the one person who has had the greatest impact on your ability, or desire, to lead?"

That's was a tough one. Only one person? Many people popped into my mind.

I thought of the really cool woman who mentored me in my undergraduate internship. She forced me to step out of my comfort zone and take risks, but completely supported and guided me.

I thought of the friend who challenged my ideas about what leadership really is and introduced me to some fabulous books and new perspectives.

I thought of a boss who gave me autonomy that I didn't appreciate at the time, but certainly benefitted from.

I thought of the bright teammate who gently, and sometimes not so gently, forced me to bring clarity to projects and goals.

Then a man came to mind. I thought of Tom Peters the author of *In Search of Excellence*, the first book about leading companies that meant anything to me. There are so many others who have taught me fabulous leadership lessons along the way and I hope I've adequately thanked you. If not, I'll get there.

But the facilitator asked for one person. OK. Being the obedient student that I am (wink), I thought and reflected on some of those who taught me a lot about leadership in more indirect ways. And unfortunately, I think I have grown the most from working with those leaders who struggle to get it right or who just get it really wrong. There's not enough room for all of those stories here, but I have many powerful lessons from the missteps of others. So, while I don't have that one person, I do have a point-of-view built out of research and experience.

BE A LEADER FROM THE SEAT YOU ARE IN AND THE SHOES YOU ARE WEARING

Though I never did settle on just one person, I will offer you the standards that I have collected along the way. I try desperately to follow these standards as I lead and consult with others who want to be the best leaders that they can be. You have the opportunity to lead every day, with a title or without. You lead and influence as teammate, a partner, a parent, a friend. So see if you can find a gem in the five leadership standards listed below. Use them to refine your style and influence people to do their unbridled best. Make your work and living environment a wonderful place, and experience the amazing outcomes that you only dreamed would happen.

- **STEP UP TO THE CHALLENGE.**

  Being a great leader is not easy, and you won't even find it easy to get ten people to agree on what being a great leader really is. That makes it even more challenging to become one. Fortunately, there are thousands of books on the subject available to you and more in the making. The bad news is that books, in and of themselves, don't have all the answers you need. Being able to espouse the latest theory, recant historical leader references, or fabricate a fable for a staff lecture does not a great leader make. Actions define leaders, so step up and live what you learn. Find opportunities to put into play the leadership advice that resonates with you. Leadership, like yoga, is a practice. It takes work, time, and some discomfort to get really good at it.

- **LISTEN TO YOUR AUTHENTIC VOICE.**

  Read, research, listen, discuss, learn, observe, question, reflect, and challenge. Then once you've gathered all of this information, write down your leadership philosophy as you see it. What do YOU really believe people need in a leader? What strengths do you embody that can be shared with those you want to inspire into positive action? What is really important to you? What are your core values? What do you want them to say about you? Answer these questions with great honesty and you'll start to create your leader voice. This voice will guide you from a strong foundation to help you take authentic action every day. Revisit this often, because once you step up, you never get to stop learning to be a better leader.

- **BE CONSISTENT.**

  You don't want to be remembered as a confusing, scattered, or inconsistent leader. Followers are looking for someone they can actually follow, even if they disagree with the direction. The best leaders are clear, forthright and, above all, consistent. As a leader, more times than not, you are trying to impart change. First, define your philosophy. Then be consistent in your style, your communication efforts, your values and beliefs. This builds trust by helping people predict how you will respond to situations and understand your expectations. When people understand and trust you, they will be comfortable following your lead into new territories.

- **BE A GREAT FOLLOWER.**

  The absolutely greatest, most impactful, and positively the most difficult, lesson to learn about leadership is to be able to follow and lead at the same time. It's incredibly important to follow your formal leader and not be a negative force. But it's equally important to follow the people you lead. In high school, I stepped up and was elected president of student council and chosen as one of two drum majors in a large band. And while I literally stood in front of the student body and the band to be in charge, it took me twenty years to learn that my real charge was to get behind and push, support, encourage. If you are successful in leading then you will be a strong force behind the people you lead. You will follow their creativity, their inspirations, their commitment, and their unique ways of getting things done. Set the direction, set the tone, set the tempo, and get out of the way.

- **BE BOLD AND BRAVE, BUT NOT BRASH.**
  Take risks. It's your job. As a mom, a committee chair, or member of a team, you need to push the limits. You need to inspire incredible ideas and encourage the outrageous. If you want to experience the best progress, and I assume that's why you are there, you have to get comfortable exploring unknown and expanding your follower's notions of what is possible. If you just want to keep things the same and safe, you might be a great manager, but not a great leader. Don't worry, if you've embraced the first four leadership standards, you can handle this! Remember, be bold and brave. But watch your style. Don't get brash or bossy. Barking orders and cracking whips are for real emergencies. Don't make situations worse by adding drama.

Remember leaders come in all shapes and sizes and are needed in all families, organizations, congregations, clubs and committees. You don't need a title to lead and you don't need to be anointed or appointed. Look for authentic actions that align with your leader-ship philosophy and allow you to follow the group you are leading.

●●

Leadership is about making others better as a result of your presence, and making sure that impact lasts in your absence.

~SHERYL SANDBERG, COO OF FACEBOOK

●●

STANDARD STRATEGY

How would you define leadership success? How do you want to be known or described as a leader? Is it all about strategy and money, or is it about the people? Brainstorm some ideas here.

Who are the three people in your life who have most influenced your leadership style and why? What specific behaviors, habits, and questions do you think made them effective? Of those, which can you embrace or build upon to make them your own.

What is the next opportunity you have to practice? What will you do? What do you expect your impact to be? What will happen?

YOUR TURN

What was the first leadership position you held? Do you think you were ready for it? Tell me about it at **https://fb.me/SuzannesStandards.**

LEARN MORE

Have you ever wondered if you have the right personality traits to be a leader? At some point in your career, you have probably taken a personality quiz or assessment and emerged with some kind of label. Maybe you were told you're introverted or extroverted.

There's an outdated idea there's only one kind of personality that makes a good leader. Usually, people think only extroverts make good leaders or that it requires innate assertive traits to be successful.

But leaders come with all kinds of styles and personalities. That's good news, because there are different kinds of leadership in the workplace and different situations call for different traits.

Some leaders need to be strategic and manage plans and goals. These kinds of leaders need to be open-minded and can get away with being less conscientious. But operational leaders, people focused on day-to-day productivity need to be less open-minded and more conscientious. And there are many other different kinds of leaders needed that require different personality traits.

So when you learn about your personality traits, don't ask yourself if you would be good or bad at being a leader. Find out what kind of leadership you do best, and then go for it.

READ MORE ABOUT PERSONALITY
AND LEADERSHIP AT
https://www.edgecumbe.co.uk/leadership-one-personality-size-does-not-fit-all/

Her Story

In my career, I've found that many different leadership styles can be effective – there is no one best way, and every employee and situation is different. Over the years, I have picked up on a common theme with leaders – both good and bad – and that is that quality of leadership is directly proportional to the quality of relationships leaders develop with their teams. I can't always recall specific events or actions my supervisors have taken, but I do remember how those events and actions made me feel.

I remember one such feeling with distinct clarity, and it has stuck with me for years. When I was still very early in my career, I was assigned to secure and arrange delivery equipment to a remote site. I worked with a wide array of engineers, operations personnel and supervisors, including mine, to determine what equipment was needed and arranged for transport to site. During this time, we were participating in daily update meetings with an audience of about twenty engineers, operators, managers, etc. Additionally, before these group meetings, I would review my updates with my supervisor to allow him to ask questions and provide feedback.

About a week after receiving the assignment, I was providing an update the group when my supervisor interrupted me to ask if I had procured a very specific item, which, of course, I had not. I responded that I hadn't, and for reasons still unknown to me, my supervisor proceeded to explain through excruciating Q&A (of which he was the questioner and I the uninformed responder) in front of the entire group that we would not actually be able to offload any of the other equipment without this item. To this day, I still cannot comprehend why he didn't mention this during any of the numerous individual or small group discussions we had prior to that moment. I have never understood why he felt the need to make this explanation to a very new employee so publicly and in such a demeaning way. Perhaps he didn't remember until precisely that moment, perhaps he thought such a public dressing down would help me not make the same mistake again, perhaps he felt I needed to be taken down a notch

I may never know his thought process. It was likely an inconsequential moment in his career, but for me, it was an inflection point. I didn't specifically think then, "When I am a, I won't..." but that moment and those feelings have informed so many of my choices as a leader. When I think of the qualities that I respect in a leader, I think of trust, of support, of authenticity. When I approach my role as a leader, I try to bring those same qualities into those reporting relationships. I work to build trust by listening, understanding and encouraging open communication within my team. I show them respect, especially when we don't see eye to eye and regardless of who is watching. I bring my authentic self every day, but I also try to consider how my approach may make people feel. Remember that your teams are made of people, and establishing trusting relationships will provide you with a solid foundation on your leadership journey.

MICHELLE BURKETT
Facilities Engineering Manager, Chevron

NOTES

You can make the choice every morning to live in the world but not be caught up in the frenzy of it, especially a frenzy of your own devising.

~SARAH BAN BREATHNACTH

STANDARD 8

Be Your Life's Editor-In-Chief

WORK SMARTER, NOT HARDER

Successful women, those who desire to stand tall, confident and stable in their stilettos, must work harder at working smarter. Gone are the days that you have to overdo it, over extend yourself, over commit, or over sweat to be recognized as a strong contributor or leader. There is a new way to approach time and energy management.

It's time to relax, focus, and apply smarter techniques for managing the demands that life presents to us. There was a commercial many years ago for dessert bars made from rice cereal and marshmallow cream – you know the ones. It was so easy to make these dessert bars that the woman hung out in the kitchen doing things she loved, while her family could assume she was working up a masterpiece. Before she brought out the dessert, she splashed water and flour on her face and pretended to look disheveled and exhausted so her family could recognize her hard work on their behalf.

We don't have to pretend anymore, at work or at home, that we have nearly killed ourselves to get something done or to engineer time to do something we love. The savvy one is the one who is resourceful enough to produce stellar results in efficient, stress-reducing ways. Build your reputation as mother, executive, cook, or technician on excellence and quality. But don't sacrifice your body and spirit in the process.

I used to dread teaching time management courses. I spent more time preparing for all the push back that participants would give me about what they just couldn't do to buy more time and the excuses they would give for not making time-saving decisions. No matter what great advice or tips I threw out, there were always those who told me that I just didn't understand what it was like to be them or to work where they work.

Around the same time, I also enjoyed watching HGTV. I know the connection doesn't seem obvious, but stay with me. As I watched the myriad of home decorating and design shows, I noticed a theme. Time and time again, designers edited their designs. They reduced their ideas and projects down to the few that would have the greatest impact. They were told to take it down a notch or adopt a 'less-is-more' approach. My time management light, which was dim, began to burn a little brighter. I formulated a new personal philosophy and a new standard for time management focusing on energy, not time. Revolutionary, huh?

Now, in my time management classes, I use the energy-management approach. I can help others reduce stress while getting better results. This approach requires a bit of a paradigm shift. To reap its benefits, we have to stop thinking of time as something to manage. After all, we cannot manufacture or purchase more time. We have to use what we have. With the exception of adjusting our clocks for daylight savings, there are and always will be only 24 hours in a day. Time is not a resource that changes its availability based on supply and demand. If fact, we have access to all there is.

The secret to self-management is learning to edit the energy we invest in our activities as opposed to managing our time. If you ever edited a newsletter, you know that there is only so much space available, so you reduce the word count. If there is a finite amount of space in your home you get rid of the clutter. If you only have a limited amount of money, you reduce your spending. It's dead simple, in theory. More difficult in real life, but absolutely possible.

I provided some parting advice to a colleague of mine when I moved on from my last job. She was a loyal, smart, capable, hardworking bundle of awesomeness. As a fan, I could see that if she wasn't careful, her strength might lead to some problems. Her greatest strength is formally defined as harmonious (from *StrengthsFinder 2.0*) and I would call it "saying yes to absolutely everything asked of her so that she didn't let anyone or any project down." If she wasn't smart about her strength, she might not get the advancement or respect that she and her contributions deserved. She might also experience physical and emotional collapse.

My advice to her was to negotiate the undone instead of saying yes to everything. This meant that she needed to be aware of her own capacity. She also needed to be willing to speak up and say, "Yes, I can do that, and here are items that will need to be removed or delegated." She took my suggestion and managed to articulate and negotiate a better use of her time and energy for better results.

BE AN EDITOR

Here are few things that you can edit in your life to help reduce the stress of trying to fit too much into the 24 hours of your day:

- **EDIT YOUR SENSE OF URGENCY.**

   Sometimes you set unrealistic demands on yourself or others to get things done. Learn to be very realistic, even generous, about the time it takes to accomplish tasks or projects. Do not impose your self-inflicted or false sense of urgency on others. Save it for real emergencies.

- **EDIT YOUR PROMISES.**

   Keep control of your commitments. You do more damage trying to please everyone and falling short. You gain more from choosing to do what you can do with grace and gusto. The results are better quality work and a better quality you.

- **EDIT YOUR NEED TO COMPETE.**

   Do you really think there is someone out there keeping score of your every move? If you are choosing to take on projects or volunteer work to beat out someone else, choose again. It's is not about winning a race or competition, is it?

- **EDIT YOUR WORRY.**

   Many of us fret way too much. Now that's a waste of time and energy. Replace fretting time with setting priorities and taking action. Take the time to determine what is really most important to you and choose to do what supports your priorities.

- **EDIT YOUR SELFISHNESS.**
  Seek help and ask for support. It is very selfish, not selfless, to not tap into the resources around you. Martyrdom is not an option on a daily basis. Your friends, family, co-workers and colleagues will edit their lives to give you a little advice, put in a little sweat, or support you. You would do it for them, right?

So now you know how to tame the wild beast we know as "time." Accept that you have all the time there is and take control of it by learning to manager your energy and edit out activities that don't meet your true personal priorities.

One fantastic source of motivation for this chapter and my own energy management is the book *The 4-Hour Work Week* by Timothy Ferris. He takes the notion of streamlining your life to terrific extremes. It is in these extremes that I think you can find ways to edit your own activities. This book will, if nothing else, help you examine your use of time. One warning, be prepared to have a plan for spending your new-found free time. I tried a few things Ferris suggested and I didn't have any activities lined up to fill my days. I found myself with too much time to fill and would pace the floor in my stilettos instead of doing something fun or productive.

It's not the load that breaks you down. It's the way you carry it.

~ LOU HOLTZ

STANDARD STRATEGY

Imagine and write down all you could do with two newly-found free hours each week. What current activity can you give up for one week to try your dream activity? How will you make this happen?

List two commitments that you have made that are not serving you well. Can you negotiate something else? Can you back-out graciously? Can you just get them done and move on? Make a plan and execute it, you will get energy just from that!

YOUR TURN

How do you edit your activities? Can you share with us your favorite time or energy-saving techniques? Visit **https://fb.me/SuzannesStandards** and let us know.

LEARN MORE

You may wonder how that one co-worker always has the energy to get things done. It seems like she has 25 hours in her day when you're barely able to get through 24. Have you ever considered getting up really early and trying to get more done? Or maybe you've tried working late into the night to help get a jump start on the next day's tasks?

No one has any more time than anyone else. And no, getting up early isn't actually the secret to making your life easier, unless you are sleeping too long. Choosing your priorities and getting support can help with an over scheduled day. Remember, edit your obligations, your tasks, and your worries.

The one thing you should not edit is your sleep. Getting enough sleep is key to keeping you functioning at your best. In order for our brains to work we need between seven and nine hours of sleep a night.

And getting up at the crack of dawn isn't the secret that will change your life. But being consistent about your bed time and wake up time just might be. When you go to bed and wake up at the same time on a regular basis, your body and mind are healthier, function better, and help you do your very best. So don't just set a morning alarm, set an evening one, too.

Learn more about the benefits of sleep at
http://time.com/money/4942543/time-wake-up-productive-sleep/

Her Story

I get my work ethic, fashion sense, and humor from my stepfather. A Clydesdale begot a Clydesdale. As the years passed by though, this horse grew tired, and I knew my strategy for work and home needed an update.

I started my professional life in nonstop, nonprofit fundraising, bought an old, temperamental home, transitioned into human resources program management, cofounded two animal advocacy nonprofits, became a cat foster mom – and as a result I started running out of time and energy. In every aspect of my life, I was working harder, not smarter.

A particularly brilliant manager of mine helped me come up with a strategy of negotiating the undone at home and at work and it has been my life motto ever since. What can come off my plate? Can I delegate? Who can help? Where/who is my release valve? Before saying "yes" to one more thing, could I truly take it on?

Initially, I felt like I was swimming against the current. I felt like I was losing control. I felt like I was failing, but after a year of practicing I feel liberated. I feel like I have room to breathe now, and I'm feeling a little more confident pushing back. One of the lessons learned for me, other than becoming my own energy advocate, is realizing that items I delegate can be a development opportunity for others – and that is a win/win.

I'd recommend negotiating the undone to anyone who feels like they live minute to minute. Sometimes, the only barrier to time and energy management is yourself. Practice taking inventory of your obligations and make your own time and energy management plan.

TARA CZEKAJ
Organizational Specialist II, Giant Eagle

NOTES

Right now someone out there is wondering what it would be like to meet someone like you.

~UNKNOWN

STANDARD 9

Weave A Strong Web

BUILD A NETWORK OF TRUSTING RELATIONSHIPS

Let's face it, we need each other. We need people. Today's women strive to be independent. But we still need lots of other humans in our lives to serve different purposes and support us in different ways. You need the friend you can call when you are upset who will give you the perfect verbal hug. You need the go-to-gal who knows exactly what to do in an emergency. You need your work friend who has a handle on every sale in every major department store. You may even need the great aunt who can share every detail about cross stitch. The relationships that we build throughout our lifetime can be the difference between success and failure, solitude and social engagement, shallow experiences and deep fulfillment.

We have a myriad of online social networking options available to us right now that put meeting other people and communicating with them right at our fingertips. There are many measurable benefits to taking part in social media. So it's worth understanding what each does and how they fit into your goals and pursuit of happiness. Currently, I use LinkedIn for professional relationships, Facebook to connect with family and friends, Instagram just because, and Twitter for a little bit of both. While I try not to miss out on the latest business and family updates, newsworthy events, or neighborhood shenanigans, I do keep my mindless scrolling and trolling to minimum. I try, and that's the key word here, to ensure that my online effort and time is meaningful and purposeful. This works for me. Be very intentional about your actions and how they support your intended brand.

Even as social media and virtual relationships grow in quantity, it's important to still build high-quality offline relationships. The old-fashioned way of putting yourself out there by attending business or cause-related events, joining clubs, taking classes, being a tourist, volunteering and even shopping still work. All provide opportunities to make a new friend or connection.

Networks, no matter how you build them, serve a social need, certainly, and provide opportunities to reach out to old friends and connect with new ones. They can also be a great and viable resource for finding potential business partners, experts who can offer advice, your new dog sitter or the mother of your future son-in-law. A network, or tribe, full of people you trust is invaluable. They can not only give you resources to enrich your life right now, but can lead you to solutions and opportunities that you can't even image right now.

Don't ever think that you don't need a strong network. It's like buying insurance. You just never know when you may need some real estate advice, to buy a special gift, to explore a new hobby, or to find the best place to eat in San Antonio.

NETWORK GUIDELINES

But, what standards should a woman follow today to allow networking to be a strong contribution in her life? Regardless of your need for networking, here are some guidelines to follow to build the tribe you can trust:

- **BE GENUINE.**

  Don't ever present yourself as anything other than you. Honesty about your reasons for networking and who you are is the only way to go. Be prepared when you approach or reach out to a new contact. This can minimize awkwardness and make it comfortable for you and your target.

- **BE DILIGENT.**

  Make networking your new healthy habit. Don't lose track of old friends or take them for granted. Keep the holiday cards going and find other reasons to make contact with and build your network throughout the year. Your biggest fans are among those you already know. Foster the relationships that mean the most to you.

- **BE CONSISTENT.**

  Don't wait until times are tough or you suddenly find yourself alone. Invest in new relationships all the time. Make it a point to meet new people every month. When you really need something, like a new job, or help with a significant life challenge, it would be nice to spend time working your network instead of building it from scratch.

- **BE CONTROLLED.**

  Don't let it consume you. There are those who weave quite a web, but reap no benefit in the long run. Set aside a set amount of energy or time and stay with it and don't become a social leech. You are going for meaningful numbers; think quality over quantity.

- **BE CAREFUL.**

  Don't abuse new or old relationships and don't become distracted by those who just want some company or are looking for the latest gossip. Extend your trust to others and be trustworthy in return.

- **BE INCLUSIVE.**

  Don't be too judgmental, or limit the kind of people you connect with. There is possibility in everyone. Look for people who have similar interests and diverse backgrounds and show up where they hang out.

- **BE GENEROUS.**

  There is an unwritten give and get rule. Never expect more out of your network than you put in. Identify what you can give to others. This is often overlooked. Invest, contribute, and offer up time, energy, your ears, your ideas. Remember that networking is a two-way street.

- **BE PATIENT.**

  You can't force anything – a sale or a friendship. Think of it like investing money. You are investing for short and long-term returns. Whatever you contribute will bring you a return, it just be might something you weren't expecting.

- **BE FEARLESS.**

  Put yourself out there, introduce yourself. Practice and be confident when approaching others. The world is full of fabulous people who are interested in meeting you. Free yourself of the shackles of shyness, go somewhere, or connect in a way that works for you.

There are many reasons to have a strong network comprised of friends, colleagues, vendors, customers and the miscellaneous. Be open to finding what needs you can have met by other people.

If you find yourself overwhelmed by thought of adding new people to your network, it's understandable. Start with a plan. Set a goal for your efforts. What is the ideal outcome? Is it as straightforward as finding a job? Is it more exploratory in nature like looking for the best place to volunteer, or is it more general, like find your tribe in a new community?

For those of you who want to become prime movers and shakers try Keith Ferrazzi's book, *Never Eat Lunch Alone and other Secrets to Success, One Relationship at a Time.*

....

In everyone's life, at some time,

our inner fire goes out.

It is then burst into flame by an

encounter with another

human being. We should all be

thankful for those people

who rekindle the inner spirit.

~ ALBERT SCHWEITZER

....

STANDARD STRATEGY

What specific needs do you have that your network might be able to help you with, right now?

Set a goal or purpose for strengthening your network. How you approach people will change based on your purpose. What do you need? A new job, business leads, money for a cause, advice? Who can help you find the person who can help you?

Is there someone from your past that you could connect with again? If so, why and when?

YOUR TURN

When have you learned something new, met someone new, as a part of someone else's network? Tell me about it at **https://fb.me/SuzannesStandards.**

LEARN MORE

Having a network of connections is different than having friends. When you're building a network, the goal is to create a web of people who can interact and support each other in their professional goals. When you're making friends, it's because you enjoy spending time together.

Sometimes these two kinds of connections overlap, and it's great. Sometimes we make the mistake of thinking someone in our network is a friend, but they aren't, and it gets awkward for everyone.

It can be hard for women to distinguish between network connections and friendships. Oftentimes, we are worried about appearing to be using people. But in a true network, it's good to make sure both parties understand it's a professional connection, and that both parties are looking for ways to succeed professionally.

This idea relates back to game theory. A strong, positive network isn't about using connections to win while others lose. It's about using connections to create wins for the group.

So don't assume every professional connection is your friend. It's ok to work together and then go home and live separate lives. But do look for those connections that help you build a strong and mutually beneficial network.

Learn more about effective networking at
https://www.themuse.com/advice/the-difference-between-networking-and-making-friends

Her Story

I was laid off for the first time in my career. After the initial shock, I realized maybe it wasn't the end of the world. After all, it gave me the opportunity to really evaluate my career and determine what was important to me. I went through all the basic steps: updating of resume, dusting off cover letters, but I knew the most important step would be networking. So I made a list of everyone I had worked with, met at coffee or networking events, went to undergraduate or graduate school with, or anyone who was in my networks or my network's network that I may want to meet.

I found the best of humanity in the process. People are innately good and truly wanted to help. The reality though, is that they didn't know how. I had a very wise individual say to me in a networking meeting, "Everyone wants to help, but you need to specifically tell them how and what you need from them." From here on out, I was aggressive, but gracious. I would reach out to my network and specifically ask, "Would you mind making the introduction for me to (fill-in the-blank)?" If I didn't hear anything, I would follow back up in a few days. Sometimes I felt pushy or that I was annoying people, but I did my best to push that feeling aside. People get busy and no one will drive your career like you will.

The power of your network can be truly amazing. It is easy to let networking go to the wayside when we get busy but this is truly how you find your next opportunity and stay connected with other professionals in your field.

MARIA VANDYKE
National Director of Recruiting, DentaQuest

NOTES

*My best success came on the
heels of failures.*

~BARBARA CORCORAN

STANDARD 10

Keep Your Eyes On The Future

BUT DON'T TRIP OVER TODAY

It was a bright, crisp fall morning and I was full of confidence and enthusiasm as I crossed the Boulevard of the Allies, one of the busiest streets in downtown Pittsburgh. I was in my black power suit and a sweet, shiny pair of stiletto boots. I was a senior consultant with a successful firm and headed to a well-known company to impart my magic on their management team. With my expert guidance, they would become better leaders and build a better organization. This was great. This was the life I wanted. This was what would lead me to a better day.

With my eyes focused on all the greatness that lay ahead, I lost focus on the moment. I took a hop-step off the curb, and I missed.

I hit the pavement. I fell down. Hard. Right there in the street in the last minutes of morning rush hour traffic with the world as my witness.

So close to perfection, and yet so far. It's ok though, because I, like you, am well-versed in getting up very quickly, plastering a smile on my face and moving on.

This misstep happens sometimes when we set goals and put energy into meeting them. We can gain some fabulous momentum. We reach some significant milestones and then, BAM, we get knocked down. There is a term that came to mind that morning while the management team was working on an assignment and I was in the ladies' room cleaning off my bloody knee. It was "hubris." Hubris is exaggerated pride and inflated confidence often resulting in a setback or failure. For me, it's a reminder that, while setting goals is a very important part of anyone's life, there is also a great equalizer in the universe. The power of setting your mind to something is real, but so is that unnamed power that will keep us humble and grounded in the current moment. Just like our physical balance when stepping off of a curb, for example.

THE REAL CHALLENGE

Setting goals is one thing, and it's a very important thing. But setting ourselves up mentally to actually reach them is the true challenge. It takes effort to step into the space in our mind that allows us to achieve a goal. We know there is a real possibility that we will get tripped up along the way. As you prepare to set or revise your goals and start the next chapter of your life with a big bang, consider these ideas for setting and achieving goals.

Set goals for yourself, not to meet someone else's expectations of you. Set goals that mean something to you. Living up to the goals that someone else has established for you may not turn out to be so great. Spend time dreaming about what makes you happy or envisioning the type of person you want to become, then go for it.

It's not always about doing more. Setting goals is not always about achieving more or climbing the corporate ladder. For you, your goal may be to remove yourself from it. Your goals might focus on de-stressing and appreciating what you already have, or finding ways to do less at work or at home to preserve your health.

- **MIX IT UP.**

  Your list of goals needs to be manageable and it needs to represent different facets of your life. Consider writing six goals: two personal, two professional, and two for family matters. This will give you a nice balance and help to ensure that one part of your life does not suffer as you work on another.

- **CONSIDER SHORT TERM AND LONG TERM PLANS.**

  You may have a long term goal of retiring in the Bahamas, or spending your twilight years on the slopes in Aspen. As you work towards those, don't neglect the quality of the life that you are living. Set some goals around your daily or weekly life that will help you enjoy what are you doing right now.

- **S-T-R-E-T-C-H YOURSELF.**

  Push beyond the normal. Reach past the obvious. Set goals that teach you something about yourself and your self-imposed limits. Whether it's learning a new language or mastering a new yoga position, there is a plethora of options out there for you. Make yourself a little uncomfortable, it does a body and mind good.

- **BE SELFISH.**

  Some people believe that setting goals can be selfish. Is being happy, healthy, focused on your current and future well-being, selfish? If so, then I say be selfish! You, of course, should not hurt or betray anyone in the process, but we have one very short life to live and setting goals to thrive is a very positive way to live it.

- **SHARE OR DON'T SHARE, IT'S UP TO YOU.**

  You might want to announce some goals to the world. Consider the guy who always referred to himself as a millionaire and one day actually bought the lottery ticket that made it so. Share with a trusted friend or two who can support you and help you stay accountable – this is great for working out. My Zumba friends expect me to be there and want a reason when I don't show up. Some goals work better when you keep them to yourself. This worked for my mom who courageously quit smoking without telling a soul.

- **REGROUP AND RE-EVALUATE.**

  The anticipation of a new year instills us with renewed hope. As each year comes to a close give yourself permission to reflect on your goals and re-write them if you want to. They are yours and if they don't rev you up or ignite renewed passion, then give yourself a re-do anytime you need to shift into a new gear, you don't have to wait for a new year.

No matter where you are in your life right now, you have not arrived. I have witnessed many people, men and women, who get the title, the big house, the power, the glory, the corner office and then just stop. They stop learning, they stop listening, they stop stretching their minds, and they stop enjoying challenges or the fun of a new adventure. Whatever you do, keep moving forward. Set your limits then push beyond. So what if you fall down? Get up and go again.

■■

I learned this, at least, by my experiment: that if one advances confidently in the direction of [her] dreams, and endeavors to live the life which [she] has imagined, [she] will meet with a success unexpected in common hours.

~ HENRY DAVID THOREAU

■■

STANDARD STRATEGY

What aspect of your life is screaming for a goal to give it focus? Take a chance, write something down and challenge yourself to see it through.

Who can you ask to be your accountability partner? Who in your network is willing to check in with you periodically to help keep you on track?

Have you set goals and failed? GREAT! Write down what you learned from a failure and then write your next goal.

YOUR TURN

How do you monitor your goals? Share with me your system and how it's worked for you at **https://fb.me/SuzannesStandards.**

LEARN MORE

I'll never forget that moment I stumbled and fell on the Boulevard of the Allies. I was set on looking ahead, I forgot to look at where I was right then and there. That moment is a literal reminder for me to be mindful.

We all lose our focus on the present from time to time. We get focused on the future, especially when we're a few days away from a big vacation. We lose track of what's going on with a big project at work because we're daydreaming of being in a beach chair, tropical cocktail in hand.

Or we are stuck in worries about the past. We can't seem to organize an upcoming event because we are still thinking about all the mistakes that happened last time. We replay the bad decisions in our head and obsess over what we wish we could change, but can't.

Being mindful is a key skill that we need to develop for success. Meditating is time dedicated to practice mindfulness. Being mindful is paying attention to what we are doing when we are doing it. It is focus and clarity in the moment, and it is essential for us to do our best work.

In order to be mindful, we do have to break some bad habits. We need to stop multi-tasking and do one thing at a time. We need to slow down and not rush from task to task. We also need to develop gratitude for our situation. Truly, being grateful is a wonderful way to do our best and feel our best.

Deep breathing and taking short breaks to help us refocus are great ways to improve our mindfulness. And don't forget to add in some exercise like I mentioned earlier. These great new habits will benefit you and your workplace. It's a win-win situation.

LEARN MORE ABOUT THE BENEFITS OF BEING MINDFUL AT WORK AT
https://www.mindful.org/10-ways-mindful-work/

Her Story

I'm big into goal setting. For me, it's a sign of progression, even if it's just a few small steps at a time. However, I can be so focused on attaining a goal, that if they're not well balanced across my life, something inevitably takes a dip. Recently, this came to a head when I found myself in the throes of a toxic work environment. Screaming colleagues, a condescending boss, taking phone calls at all hours of the night. It was less than ideal.

I contacted Suzanne to re-evaluate my situation. I wasn't feeling fulfilled in my job and was having a hard time seeing the next step. She had me do a core values exercise, and I gave it a try, but I did so begrudgingly. It seemed fluffy to me. But that's when the aha! moment came. When I started, I sunk my teeth into each of the questions and appreciated the depth of what the exercise embarked on. Never doubt an expert!

After an hour or so, I was left with my top five core values. Of course, I knew the traits I valued and admired, but never before had I had a succinct list of words that really summed up what I was all about. I spent several days doing the exercise and taking stock into all areas of my life. What really aligned with my true self and what didn't? It became glaringly clear which areas weren't serving me. New goals, this time much more holistic, followed suit.

I keep my five core values on a note in my phone: family, health, joy, independence and belonging. When I'm on the fence about something or considering tackling a new goal, I pull that up. It's usually pretty easy to discern if what I'm considering doing will align with who I am.

In a world that praises hustling and stress, I found uncovering my core values reframed my thought processes and goals. I began putting up healthier boundaries, making small networking goals (get coffee instead of navigating an auditorium size room of strangers) and perhaps most importantly, began appreciating that although I wasn't exactly where I wanted to be, I was learning a whole lot on my way there.

MICHAELA H. ROBBINS
Regional Director, Core Realty

NOTES

···

I can do that.

I should be allowed to do that.

~GLENN CLOSE

···

EPILOGUE

I struggle, as I think many of you might, with what it means to be a successful woman or a feminist today. The feminist movement, like so many other evolutionary metamorphoses, will ebb and flow in its intensity, its clarity of purpose and its effectiveness. As we ride this wave of purpose and emotion, I hope women can lift their heads and see the big picture and balance the desire to impart change with patience for one another, including men. It took thousands of years to build the social norms that frustrate us and hundreds of years to pass the laws that were designed to help us. We have come far, but it will take more time, let's hope not too long, to experience the full impact of this vital work.

Whether you are a feminist or not, confused or not, I hope you found value in these ten standards. And I hope that you can lift some ideas and inspiration to define and realize your own success, whatever that may be.

Thank you for reading my little contribution. Share what you learned and like with others. And always do your part to help those around you be better.

WHAT COMES NEXT

As an individual, you can do a lot to define and create your own success. But our organizations and businesses have a responsibility to create and sustain environments that make success possible. Here are six key actions organizations need to embrace for a respectful and successful workplace:

1. *Set targets for gender equality. Report on progress and be held accountable.*

2. *Institute fair hiring and promotion processes.*

3. *Ensure that senior leaders lead by example and champion diversity.*

4. *Create an inclusive and respectful workplace. Work to identify and eliminate micro-aggressions, subtle signals of disrespect. These negative comments, assumptions, and slights add up.*

5. *Make the "Only" experience rare. (An Only is the only woman, or the only person of color, or other aspect of identity, in a certain department or at a level of management.)*

6. *Offer flexibility and support a work/life balance.*

Is your workplace offering individuals the best chance to succeed? How are these bad policies and behaviors holding the entire group back? What can you do to work for positive change?

READ MORE ABOUT THE WOMEN IN THE
WORKPLACE 2018 STUDY CONDUCTED BY
MCKINSEY AND LEANIN.ORG AT
*https://www.mckinsey.com/featured-insights/gender-
equality/women-in-the-workplace-2018?cid=eml-web.*

LEARN MORE ABOUT HOW I HELP
ORGANIZATION TACKLE THESE IMPORTANT
ISSUES AND REALIZE GREATER
PERFORMANCE WITH AN INSPIRED
WORKFORCE. VISIT
www.weinspiretalentsolutions.com

ABOUT SUZANNE MALAUSKY

Suzanne is CEO of WeInspire Talent Solutions, a talent management consulting company located just south of Pittsburgh, PA. Suzanne has been inspiring others to do their best for over 20 years. From the intimate setting of an executive board room, to the expansive experience of an auditorium, she brings her consulting, corporate, health care, human resources, leadership experience and insights to her customers and audiences in a straight forward, keenly relatable way. She is the proud mom of two awesome, high-functioning adults, Abbe and Drew, the bonus-mom to 2 smart, fun-loving kiddos, Cole and Maliah, and the lucky wife of a strong, patient, loving, and kind man, Michael.

INSTAGRAM *@SuzannesStandards*
TWITTER *@SuzannesStandards*
FACEBOOK *SuzannesStandards*

VISIT *www.weinspiretalentsolutions.com*
to learn more about Suzanne and WeInspire Talent Solutions.